AF430482

Mermville

Jeanne' Kirkpatrick

Dedication

I dedicate this love story to my grandchildren, McKenna, Connor, Jack, Zahara and Cameron. Also, to all the children in the world, and young at heart people. Be open to love at all time and find compassion inside of your heart. Be kind and be gracious to everyone. Share your love openly.

Bless the children and mankind.

I hope you all grow up with love surrounding you. Take your time in life and see the opportunities that come your way.

Do not forget to hug the trees and smell the flowers along your path, as they are sending you love messages.

Acknowledgment

I want to acknowledge the people who gave me their undivided support and love in creating this children's love story.

My daughters, Melissa and Jaime, my good friends, Pat and Ross Hallberg. My artists, Emma and Peter. Thank you for all the hard work you created. My friends who were supportive of this adventure. Suni Tafoya, Laura Constantine, Jim Hague, and my long time BFF, Jan Venturini. My partner, Dennis Rossman, whose daily encouragement, and constant inspiration he gave to me with love and joy,

I thank God, my angels' guides, ancestors and the divine who made this book possible.

About the Author

Jeanne' was born and raised in an Mateo Ca. A nice childhood lead to recognition as a world record track star at the age of 13 years. Jeanne' has also won awards for her artwork. She later became an interior designer working for furniture stores and creating her own business. The storyline was channeled to her and Jeanne' created the characters from her grandchildren and their personalities.

Jeanne' is retired and enjoying her quiet lifestyle with her partner.

In the land of ESS, where beautiful flowers grow, where the fragrance fills the air, where bees, butterflies, and birds gather nectar, there lives a family of worms under a tree.

The members of the Merm family are Poppee Merm, Momme Merm,the twins Jack and Miss M, and Baby C.

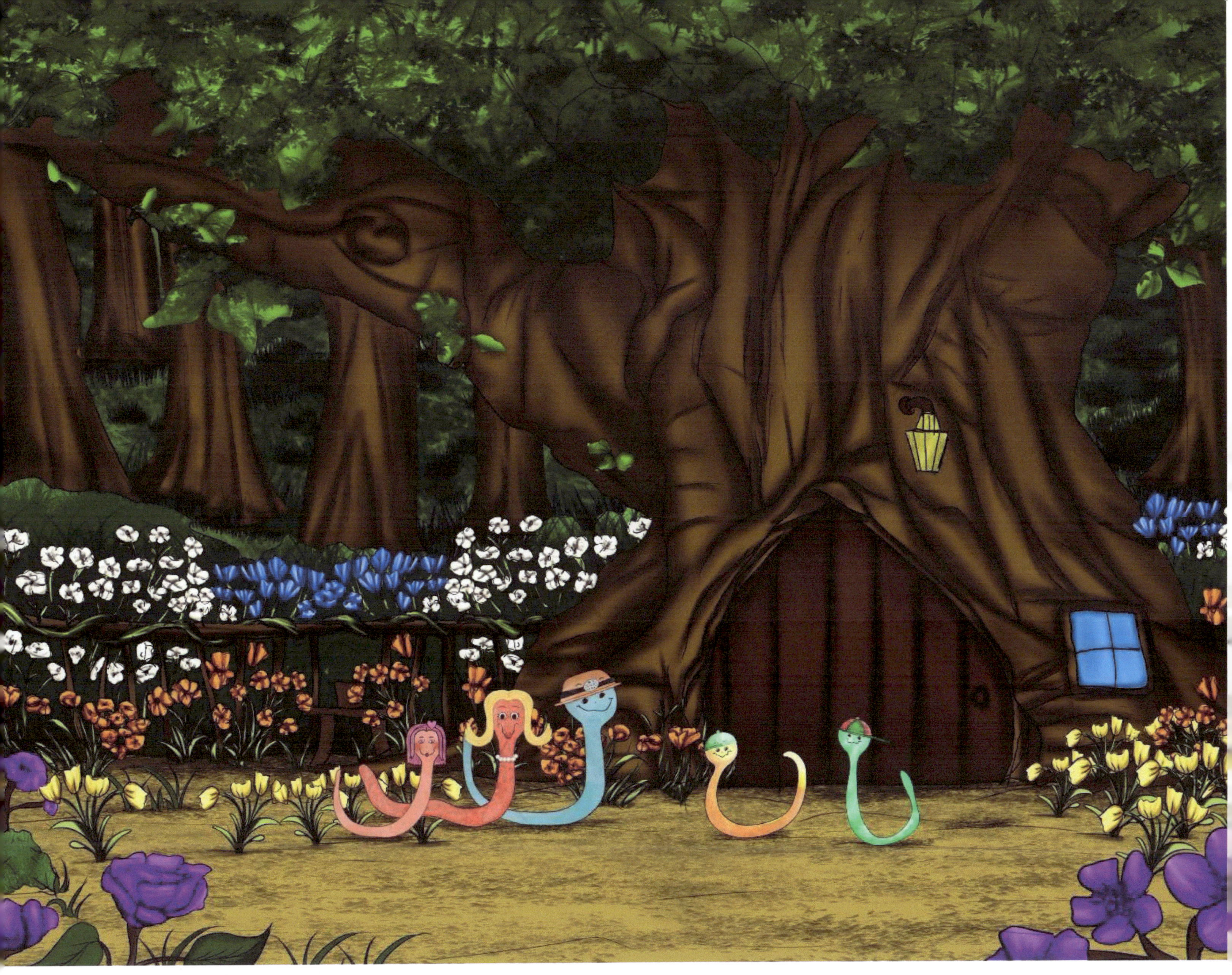

Gramme, Grandpa Merm and Auntie Meme Merm live nearby.

Baby C is the newest Merm family member. He was born in the shape of a C. He cannot crawl in a straight line. He scoots along the ground, leaving little mounds of dirt in his path.

The Merm family, along with a community of worms, nurtures the soil for the flowers to grow and bloom in the gardens by digging holes and tunnels.

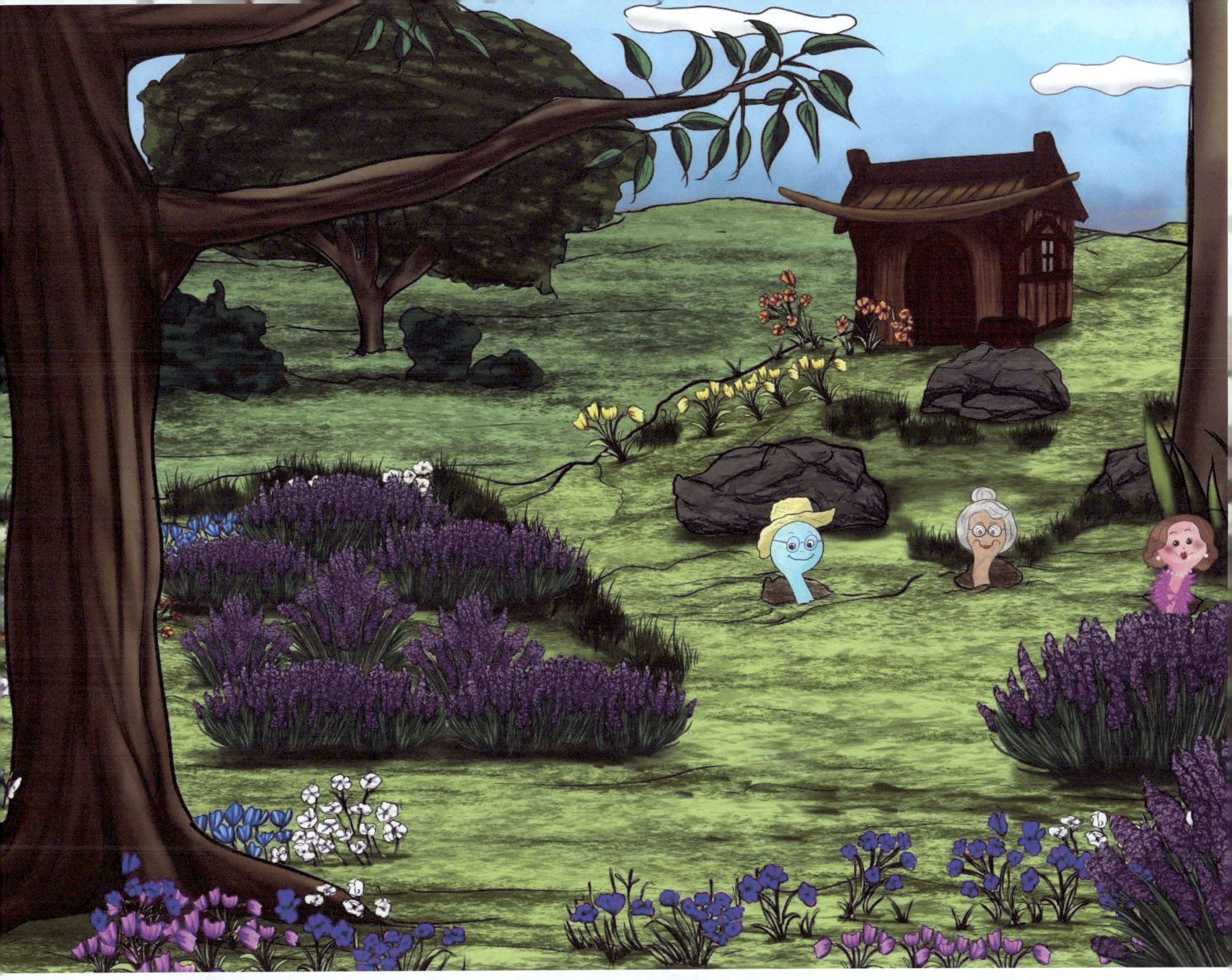

This allows the bees, butterflies, birds, and other nectar-gathering insects to feed on the nectar. The insects move to each flower in the garden and spread pollen to each flower. Viola! More flowers.

The real reason the bees, butterflies, birds, and insects visit the flowers is to listen to the secret love messages shared by each flower. They travel from one flower to another, listening and sharing these daily love messages. These messages are shared with every creature in the village.

Every morning Zahara butterfly is first to the garden. Zaahra uses her front legs to find the sweetest flowers.

Zahara shows the waiting Buzzy Bee sisters MM & JJ where to start to gather the fresh nectar.

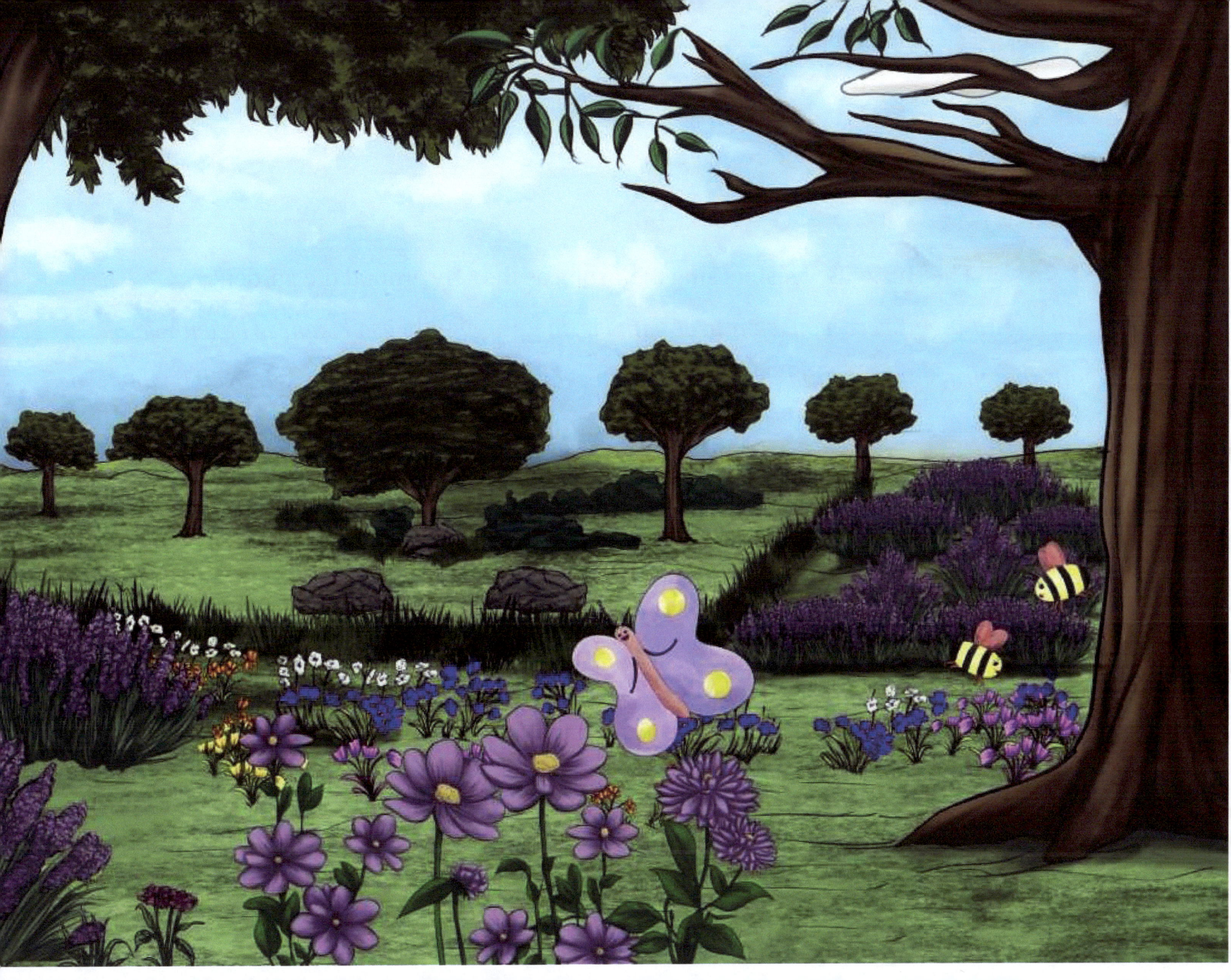

The Buzzy Bee sisters sing their song as they fly around the garden:

"Higgity-biggity bee, you want to be with me, higgity-biggity boo I want to be with you. Higgity-biggity bee, come and follow me, and we will see what we can see, oh we'll be what we can be. So, come and follow me."

Sometimes, JJ becomes excited and flies fast to drink the nectar too quickly.

JJ flaps her wings so fast that the nectar sticks all over her body, and she becomes stuck on the flower petals.

Mm helps JJ with the sticky mess down to the table in the nearby park. The nectar has turned into sweet honeycomb candy!

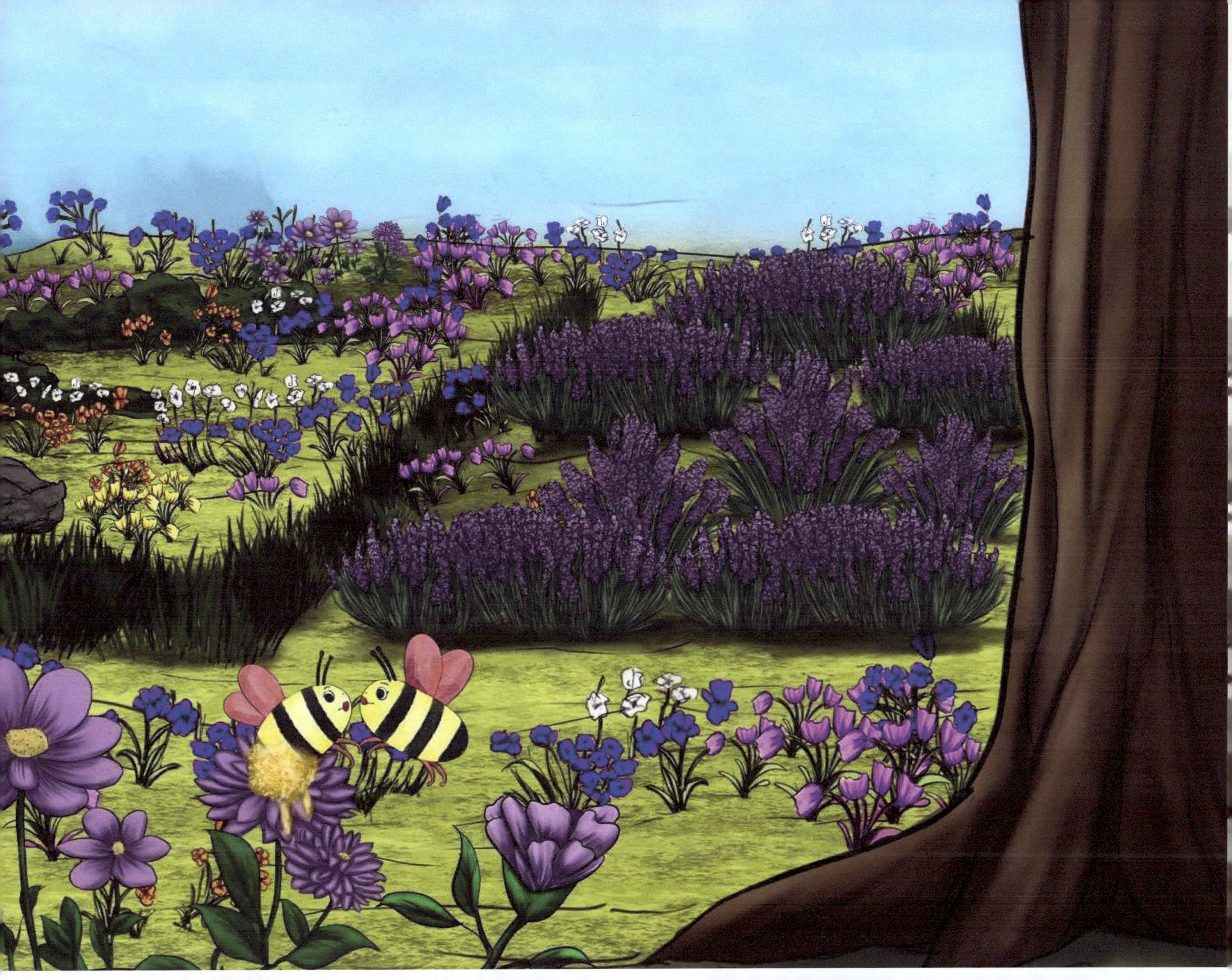

"Let's share the candy!" They put the candy on the table for all Mermville critters to enjoy. Happiness!

Jack plays sports with his friends in the park. They love to play hide and seek.

Jack helps Grandpa Merm make all the rides for the playground. The Mermville critters gather flower petals, feathers, leave, and stems to create playground rides and costumes for plays in the park.

Auntie Meme Merm often visits the playground wearing her long boa of feathers and jewelry. She teaches the critters about acting. They put on plays and performances on the stage in the park.

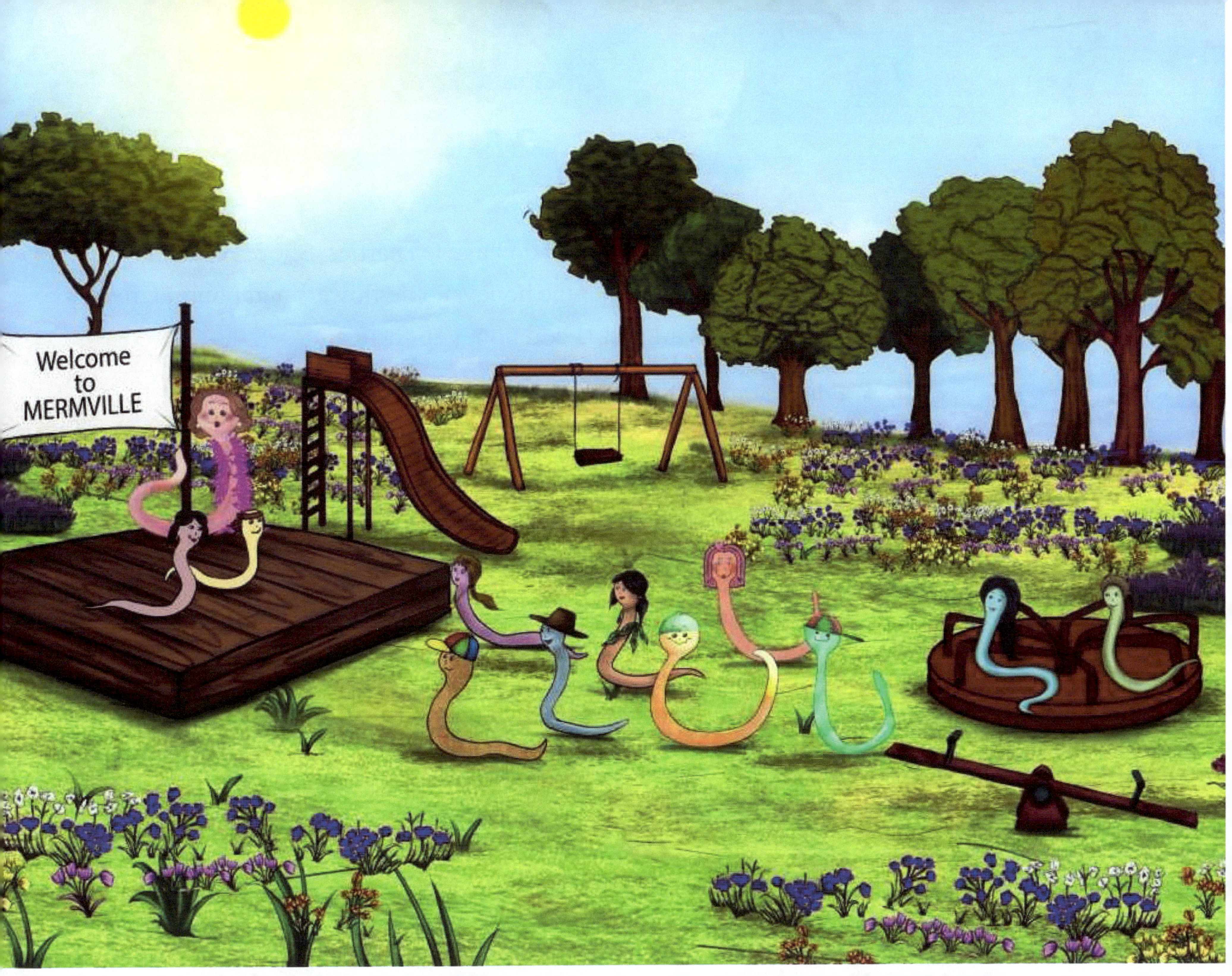

Welcome
to
MERMVILLE

Miss M loves to play dress-up with her friends and have tea parties. She loves to make honeysuckle tea. Miss M and her friends gather the honeysuckle flowers and pour the nectar into a teapot. MM and JJ add honey to the tea.

They gather at the table and sing a special song: "*Honeysuckle tea*

made just for you and me, jus for you and me.

We all sit here drinking our honeysuckle tea.

We all love our Honeysuckle tea."

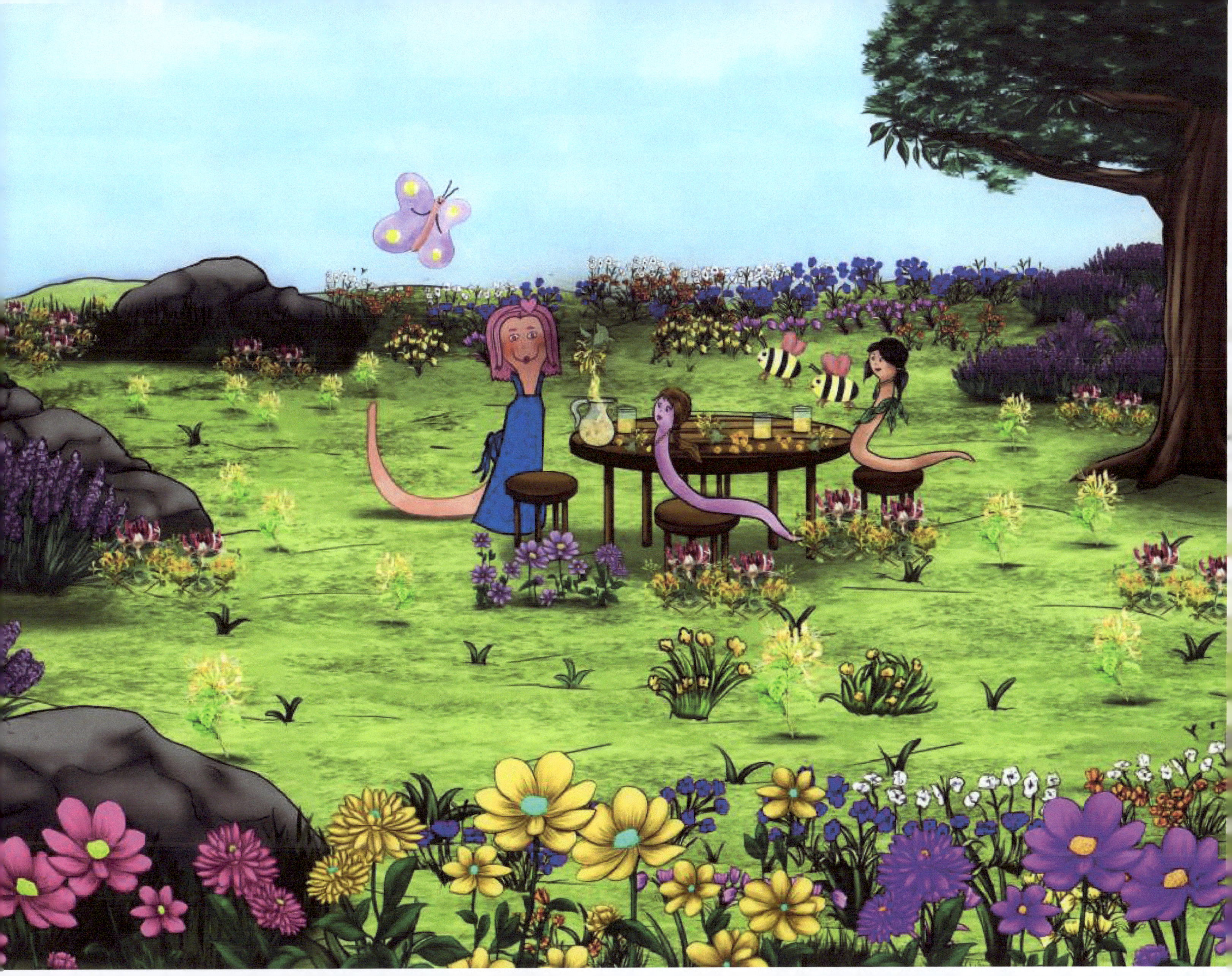

One day Miss M and her friends were gathered at the table enjoying the tea and treats. They left to watch Jack play baseball.

When they returned, they noticed the tea and treats were gone. They did not know what to think about this. They began to look around at the nearby flowers.

Suddenly, they noticed a moving eye in the flowers! "What is this?" They saw a figure in the flowers. They said, "Who are you?"

The creature crawled down from the flowers.

"Hello, I am lost. My name is Cameron, the Chameleon. I saw this delicious food and tea on the table, and I was so hungry I just had to eat it."

The critters felt so bad for Cameron and invited him to stay and be a part of the community.

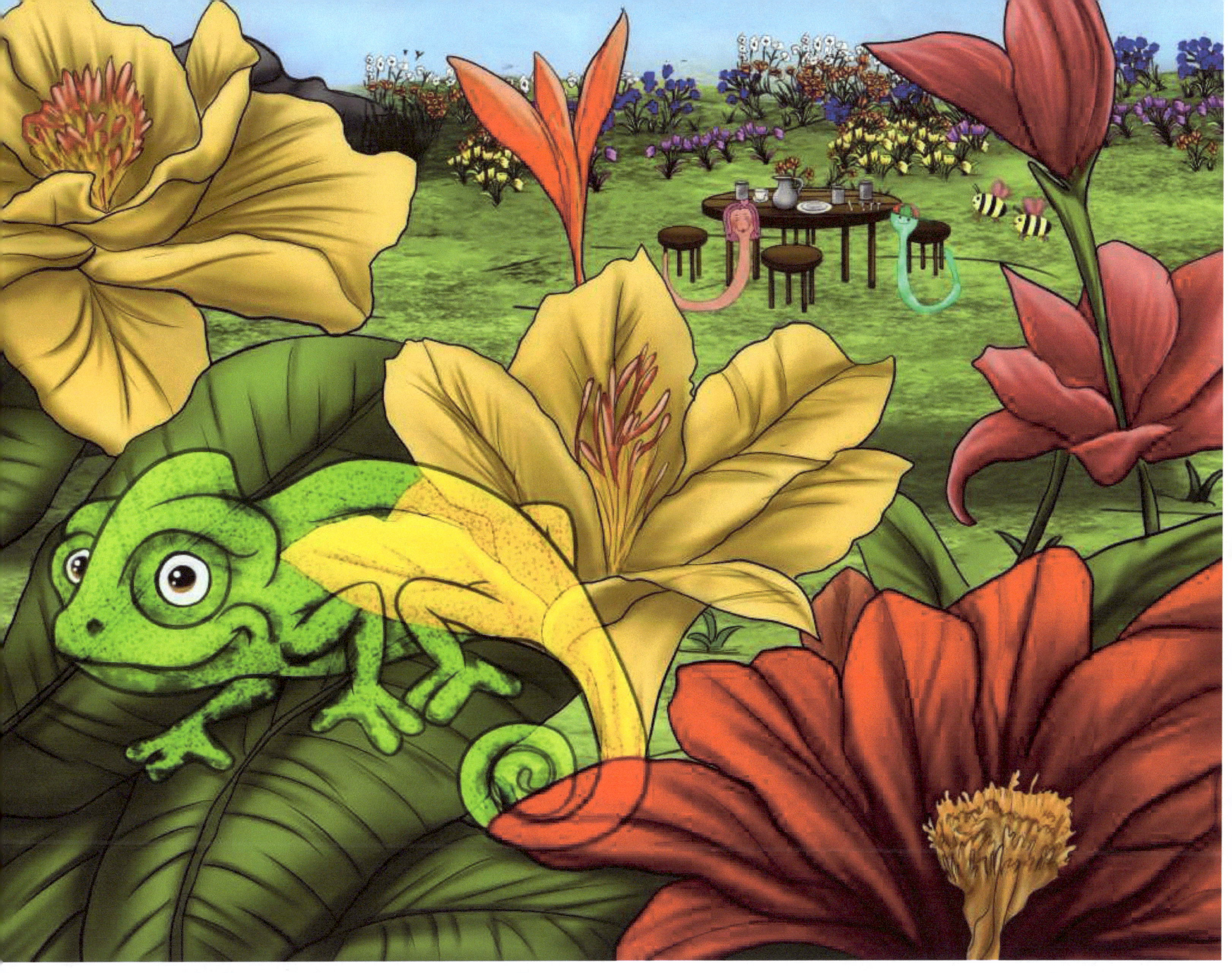

One day, Poppee Merm noticed Mermville was growing bigger.

Poppee gathered some of his friends and traveled along the path to the other side of the park.
Poppee was looking for land to expand the village.

They decided to start building the village on their side of the berm next to the park.
They saw tractors, trucks, and backhoes digging up the dirt. It was noisy.

Momme Merm began to prepare for the move to the new area.

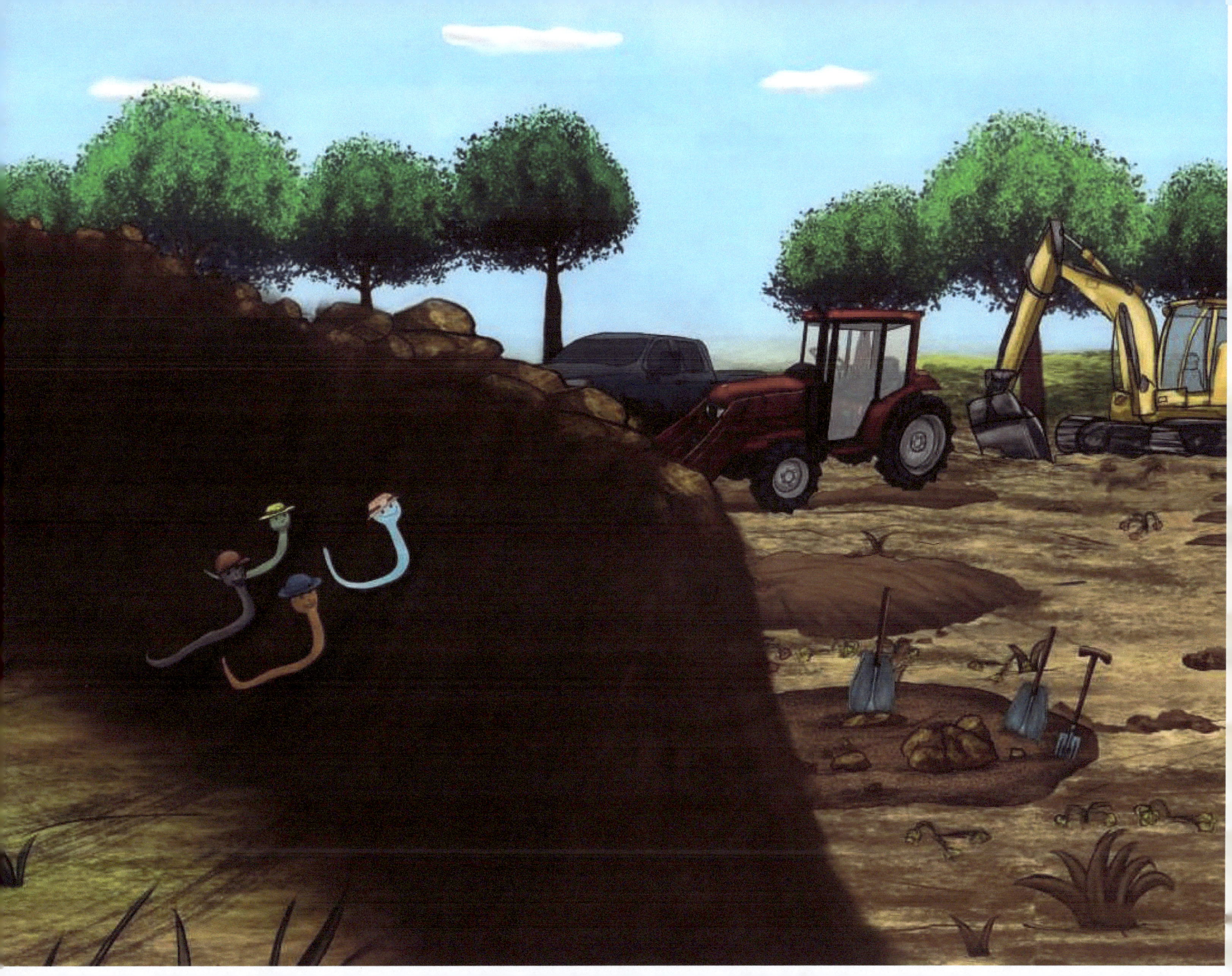

Meanwhile, Baby C was scooting along the path, and the twins were to watch after him.

Miss M and Jack saw the other critters playing in the park and went to join them.

They forgot about Baby C.

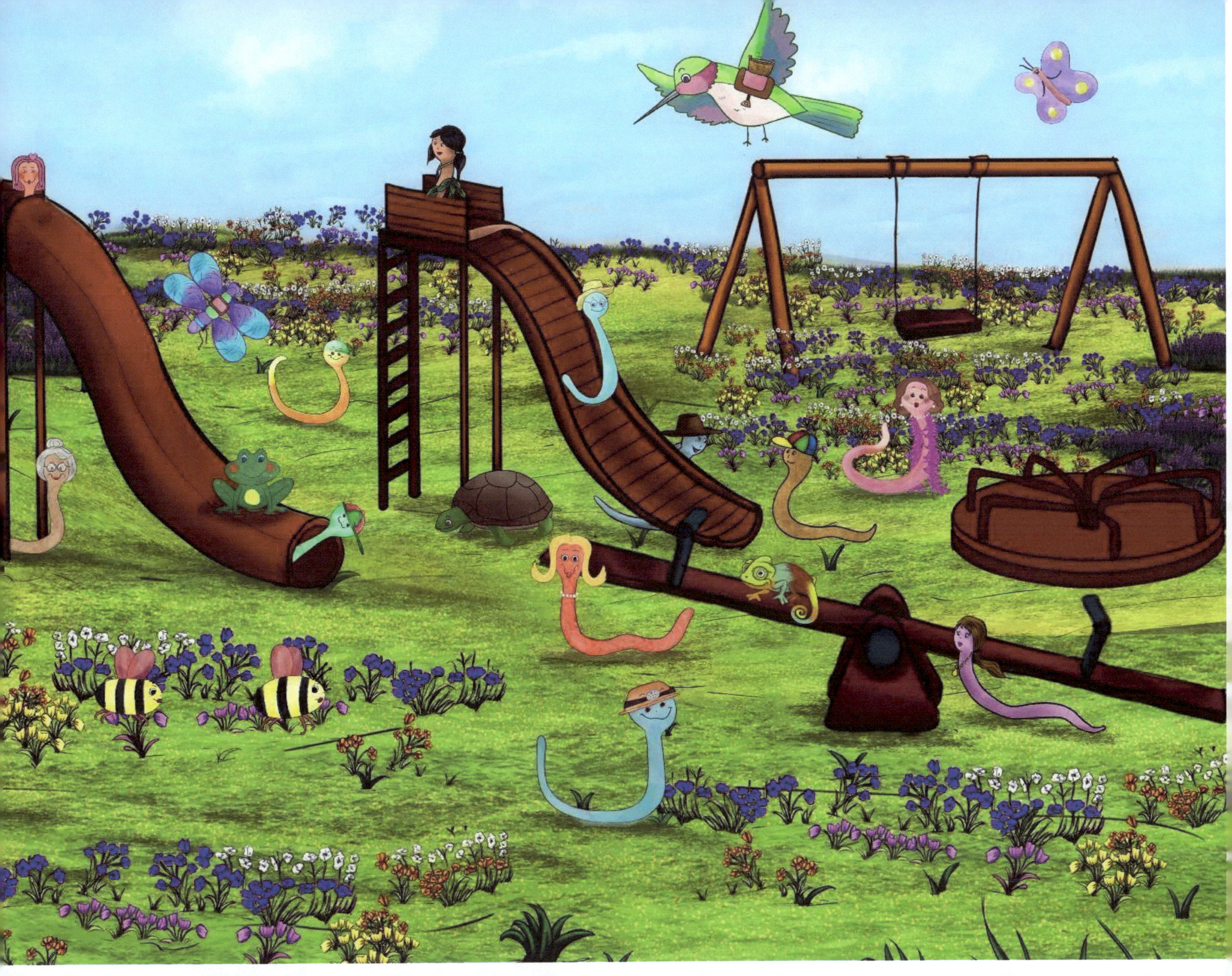

Baby C crawled close to the edge of the path, tumbled down, and landed by the pond where Franne Frog and Tillie Turtle were watching this happen.

When the twins could not find Baby C, they alerted everyone in the village to help find him.

Franne Frog began to croak to alert the community that she was with Baby C.

Tillie Turtle stayed by Baby C to comfort him as he had bumped his head on a rock and was scared.

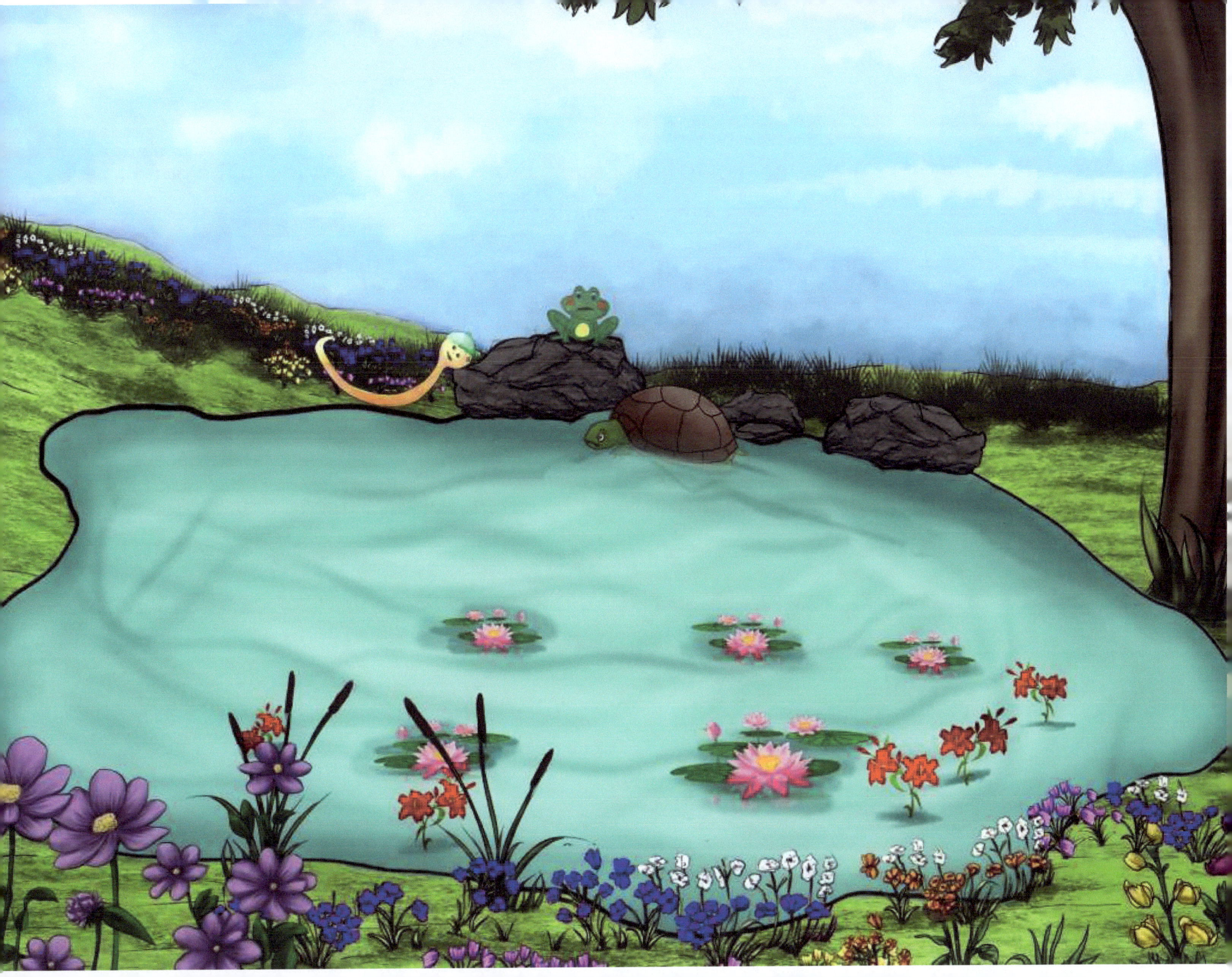

Darren, the Dragon Fly, was the first to hear Franne Frog and came buzzing to the pond to see what the matter was.

Darren flew to tell Hummy the hummingbird because he could fly faster and had a bigger saddle to carry Baby C to safety.

Darren gives rides to the critters of Mermville. The critters crawl up on the tallest flowers and climb onto his saddle. Darren flies them all around the village.

Darren sings his song as he flies around the village:

"Darren is always starrin and the many possibilities. Darren is always starrin with his many eyes that see.

Cause Darren is always starrin at the many places he can be.

Darren is always carrin about you and me".

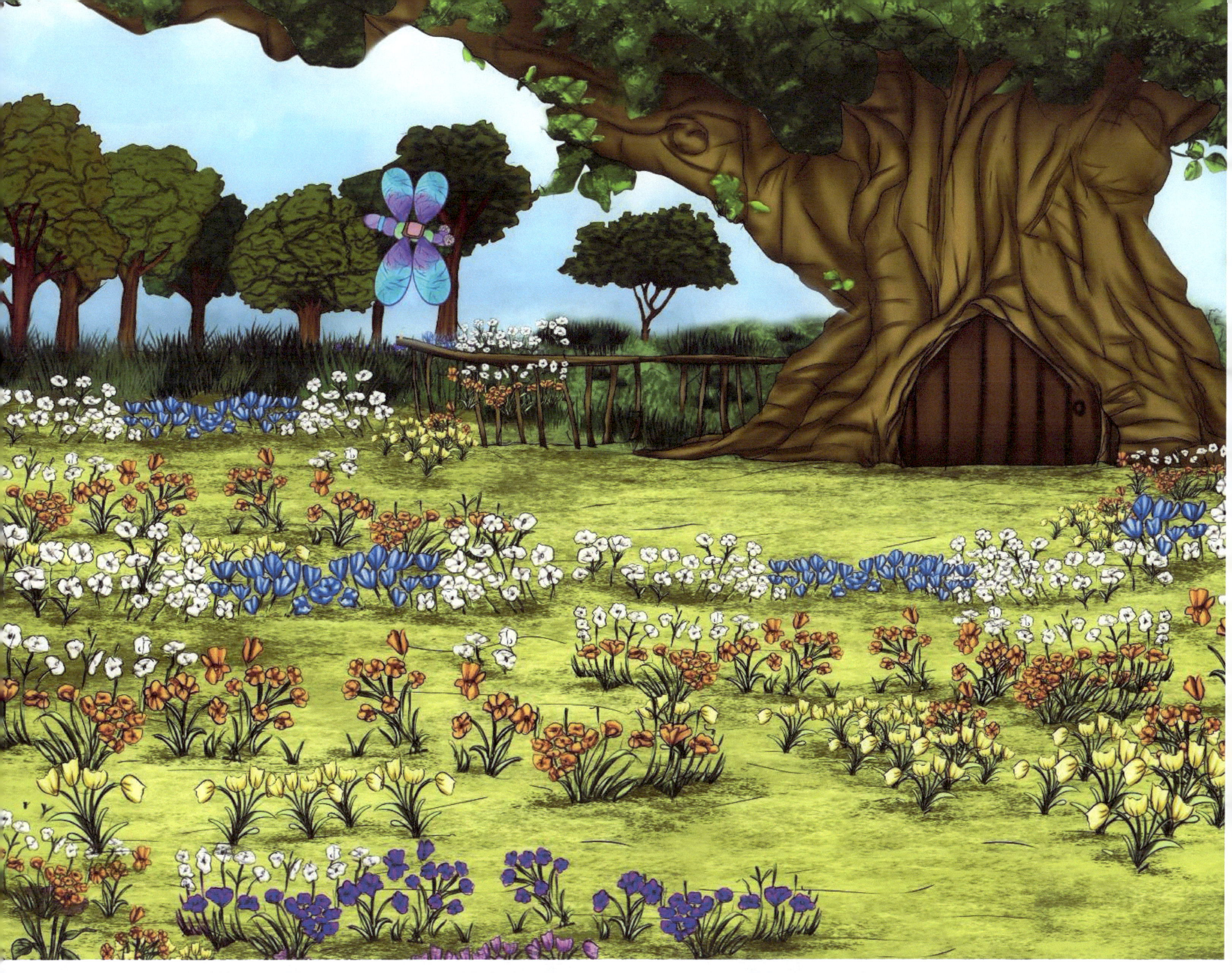

Hummy is very fast because he must drink nectar 4 times his weight every day!

Hummy immediately flew and gathered up Baby C in his saddle. He flew Baby C directly to Gramme and Grandpa's house.

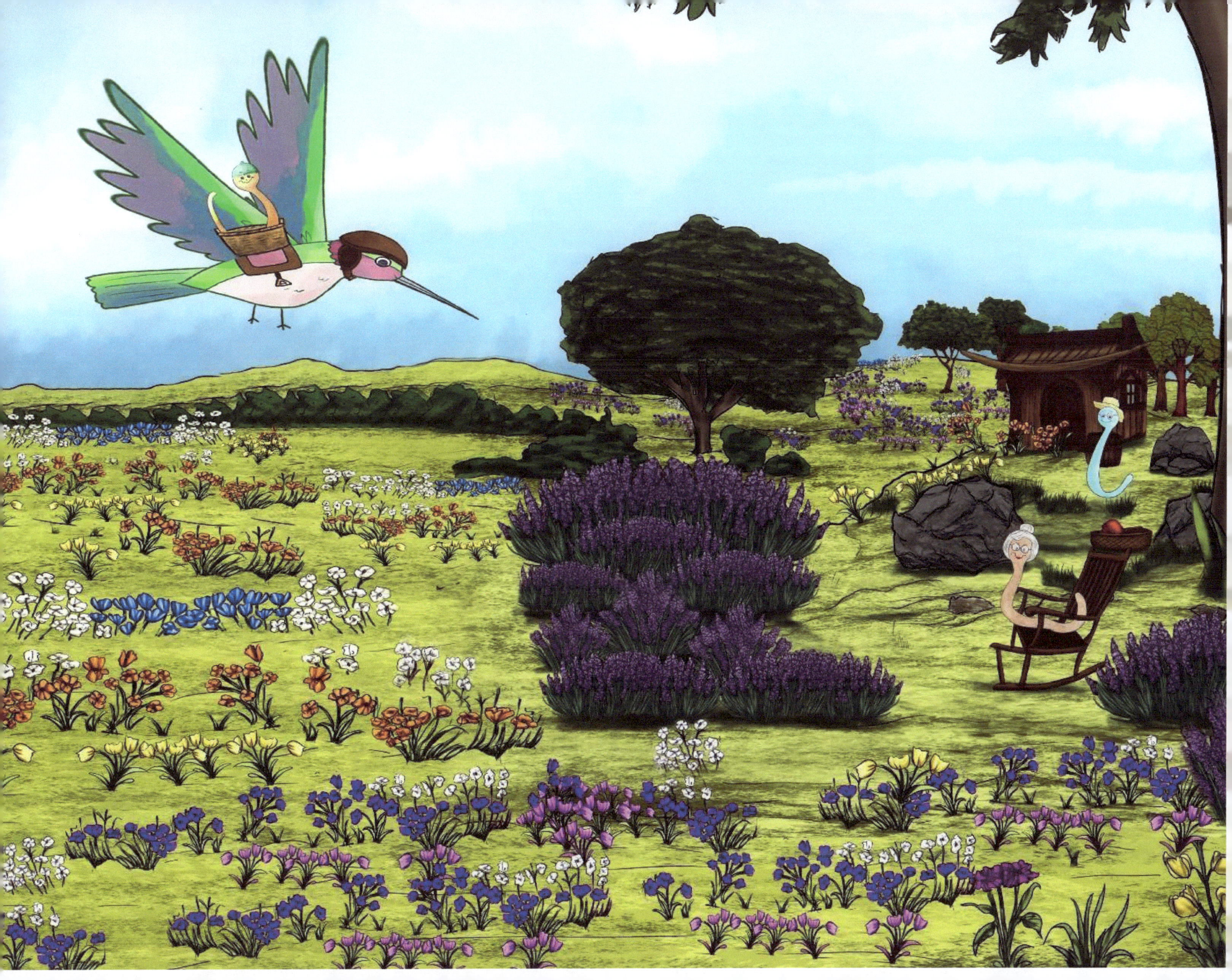

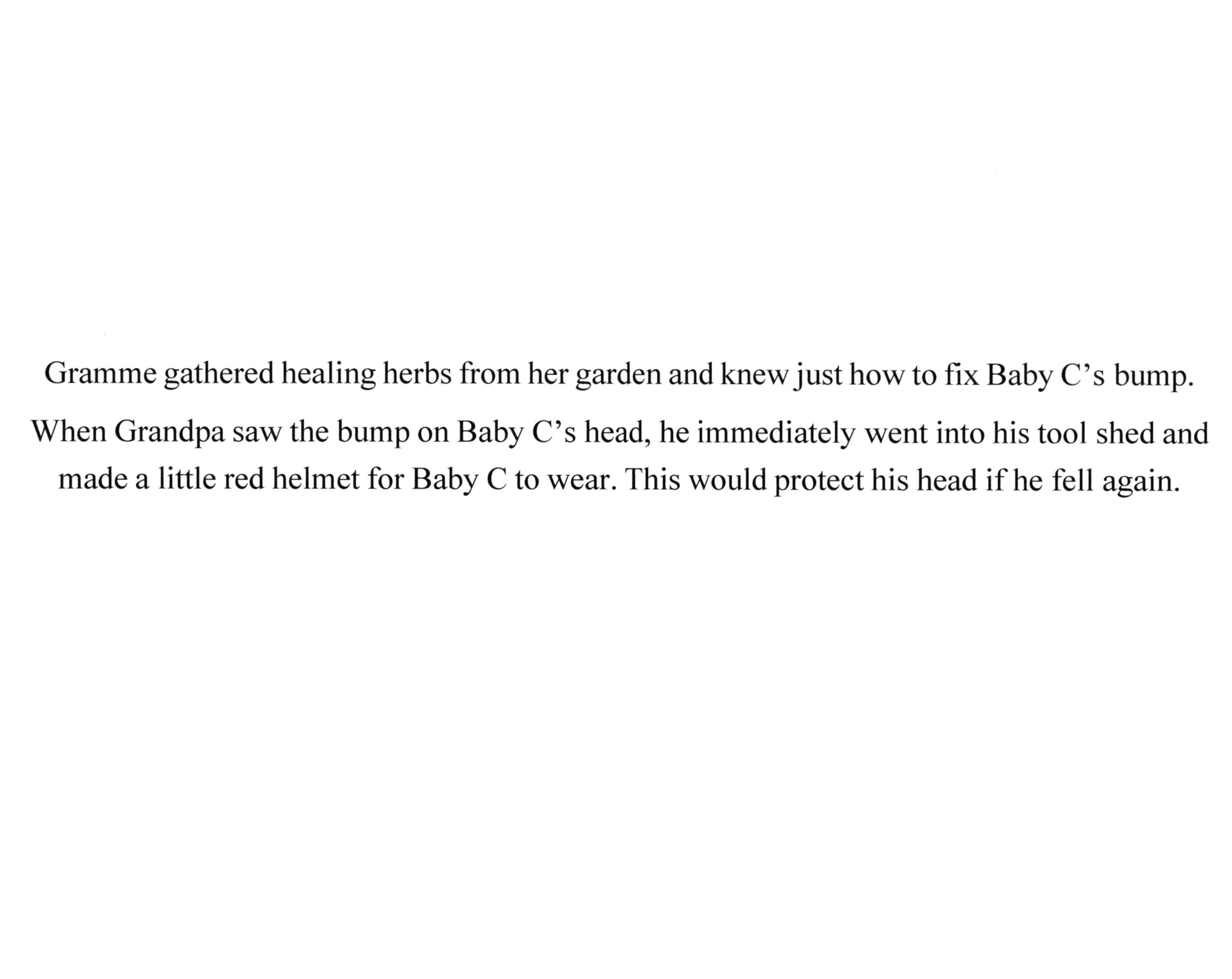

Gramme gathered healing herbs from her garden and knew just how to fix Baby C's bump.

When Grandpa saw the bump on Baby C's head, he immediately went into his tool shed and made a little red helmet for Baby C to wear. This would protect his head if he fell again.

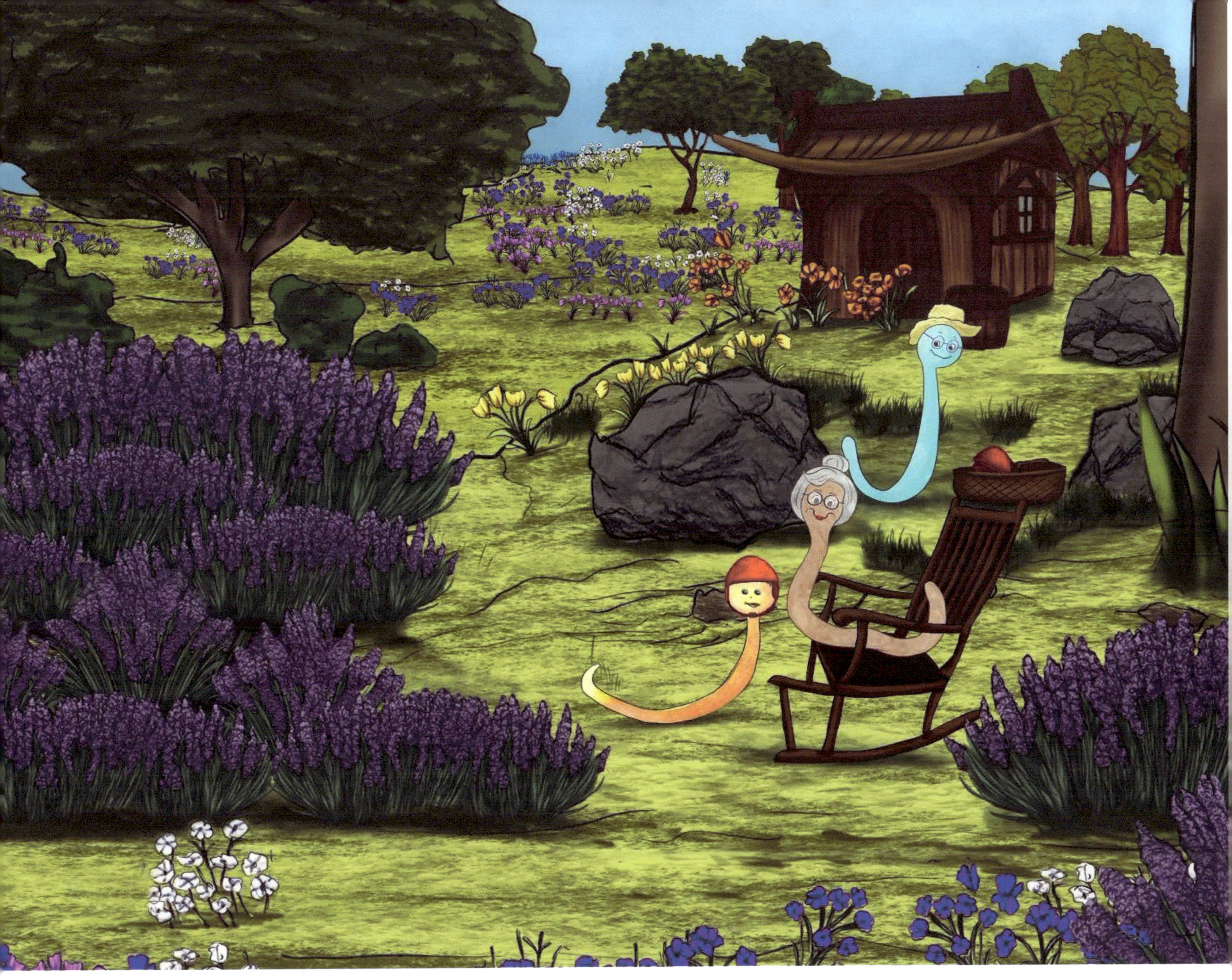

Meanwhile, Poppee Merm and his crew began to prepare the new land by burrowing into the soil so the flowers would grow.

Baby C wanted to help and would leave little mounds of dirt as he moved along the path.

Everyone was busy preparing for the new land.

One day, the wind started to blow. It blew all the seeds that the tractors had piled up on the other side of the berm into the holes the worms had dug and into the mounds Baby C had made.

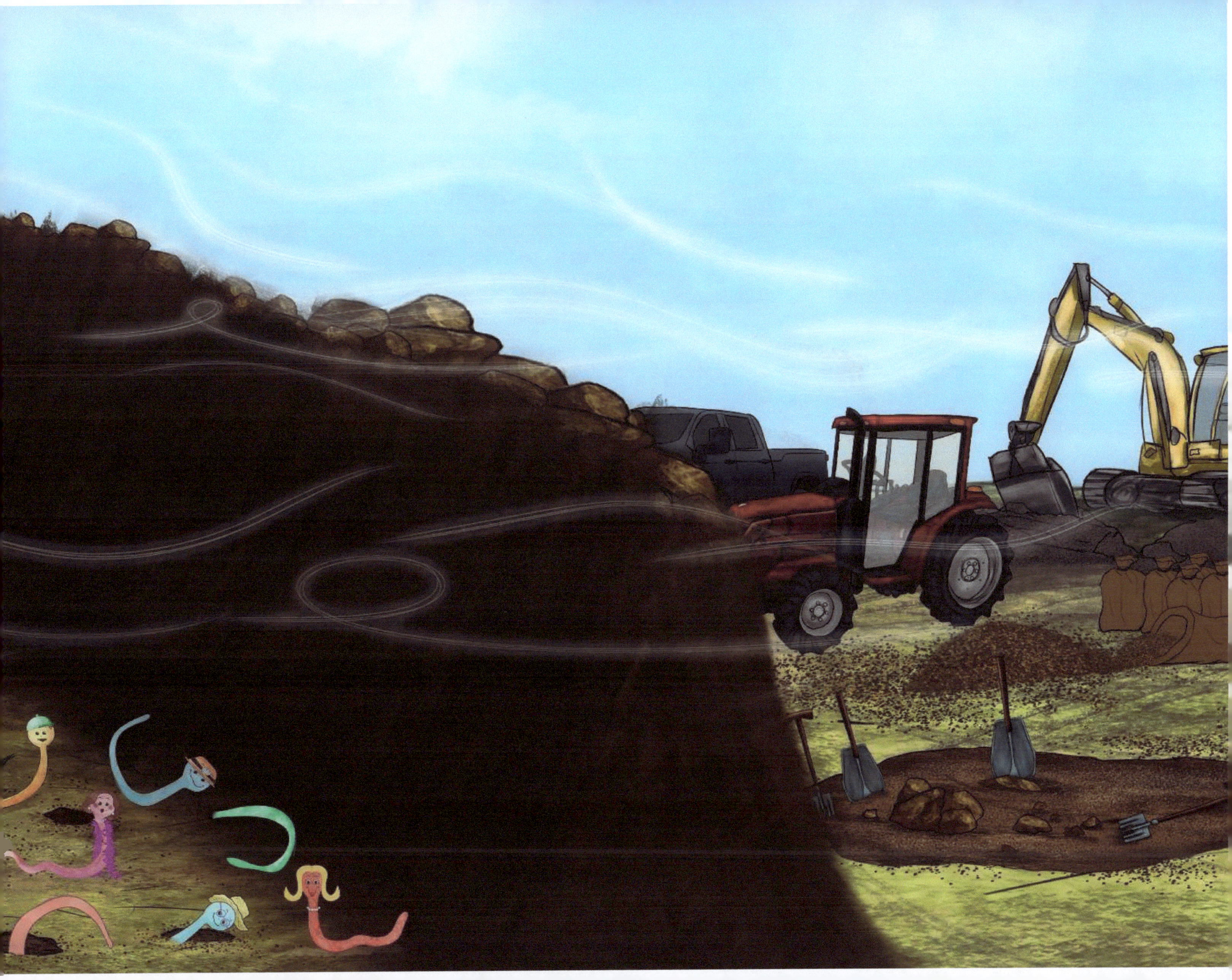

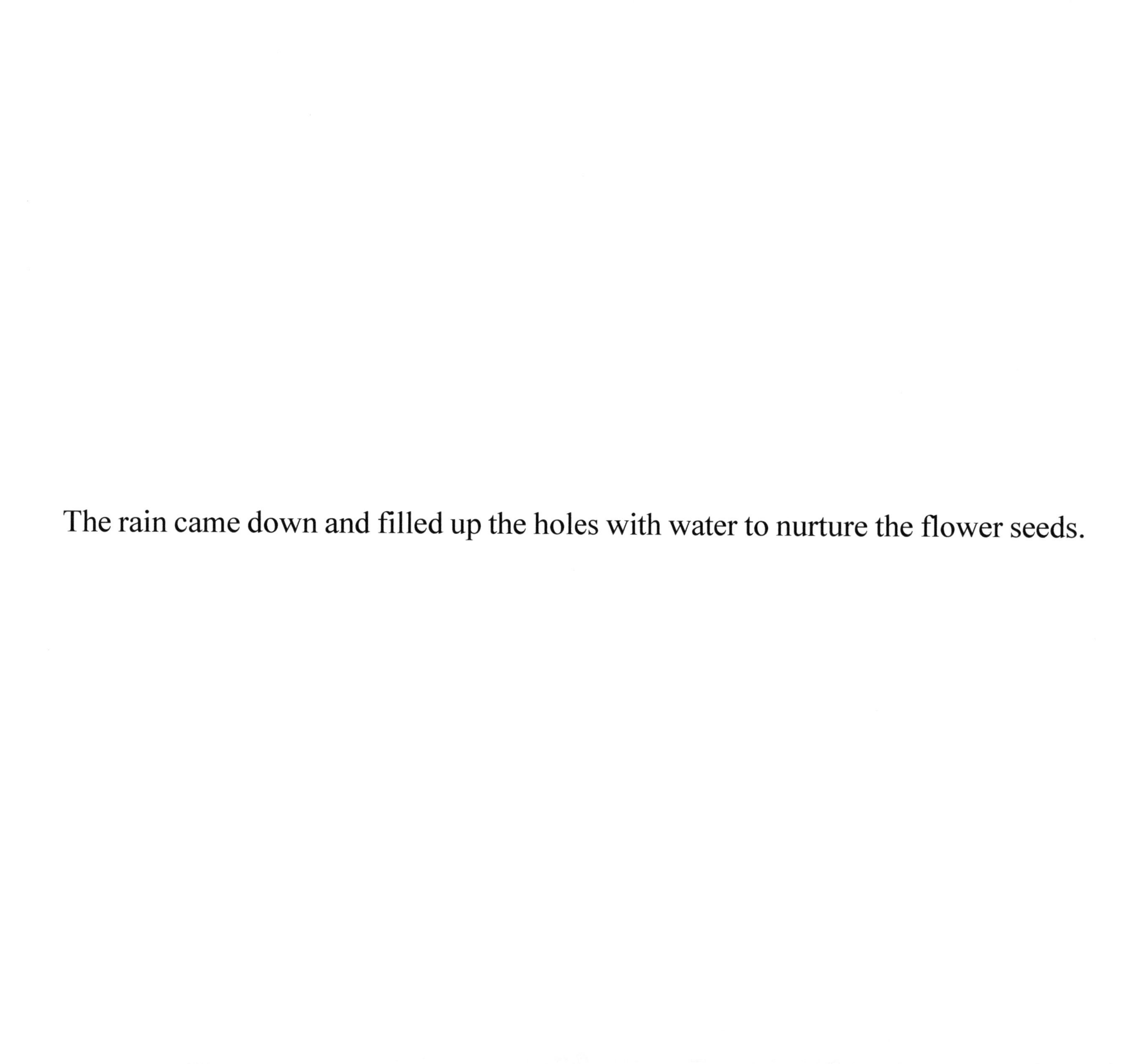

The rain came down and filled up the holes with water to nurture the flower seeds.

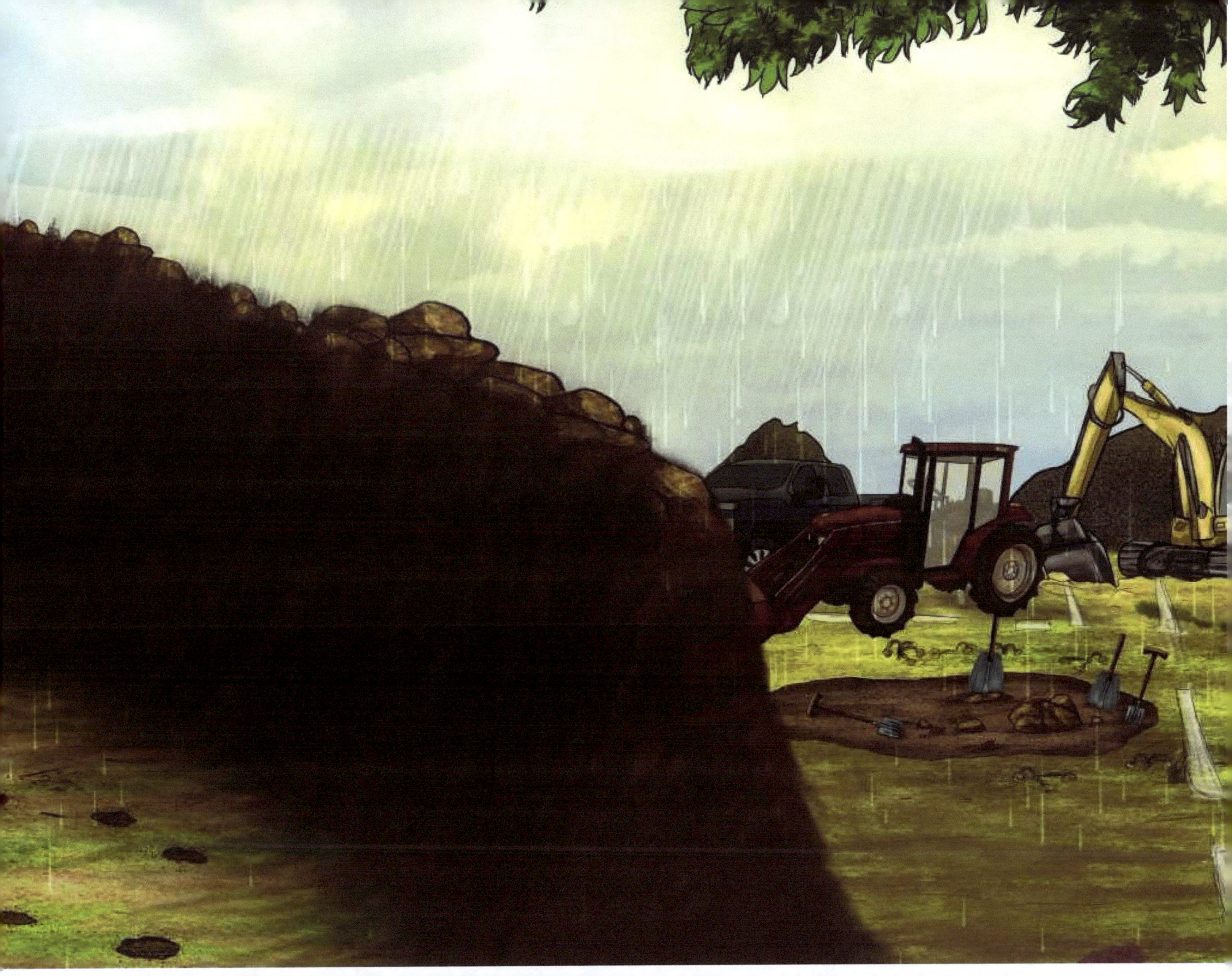

The Sun came out and warmed the soil, which made the little seeds grow into plants.

In a few months, the plants had grown tall, and the flowers bloomed in the new garden.

The community was a buzz with insects gathering nectar from the flowers and listening to the love messages that were shared.

Everyone in Mermville was happy that they had a bigger village.

Mermville critters were curious about what happened to all the noise from the tractors on the other side of the berm.

Everyone wanted to celebrate the new space they had created. They all crawled up to the tallest sunflowers to look over the berm.

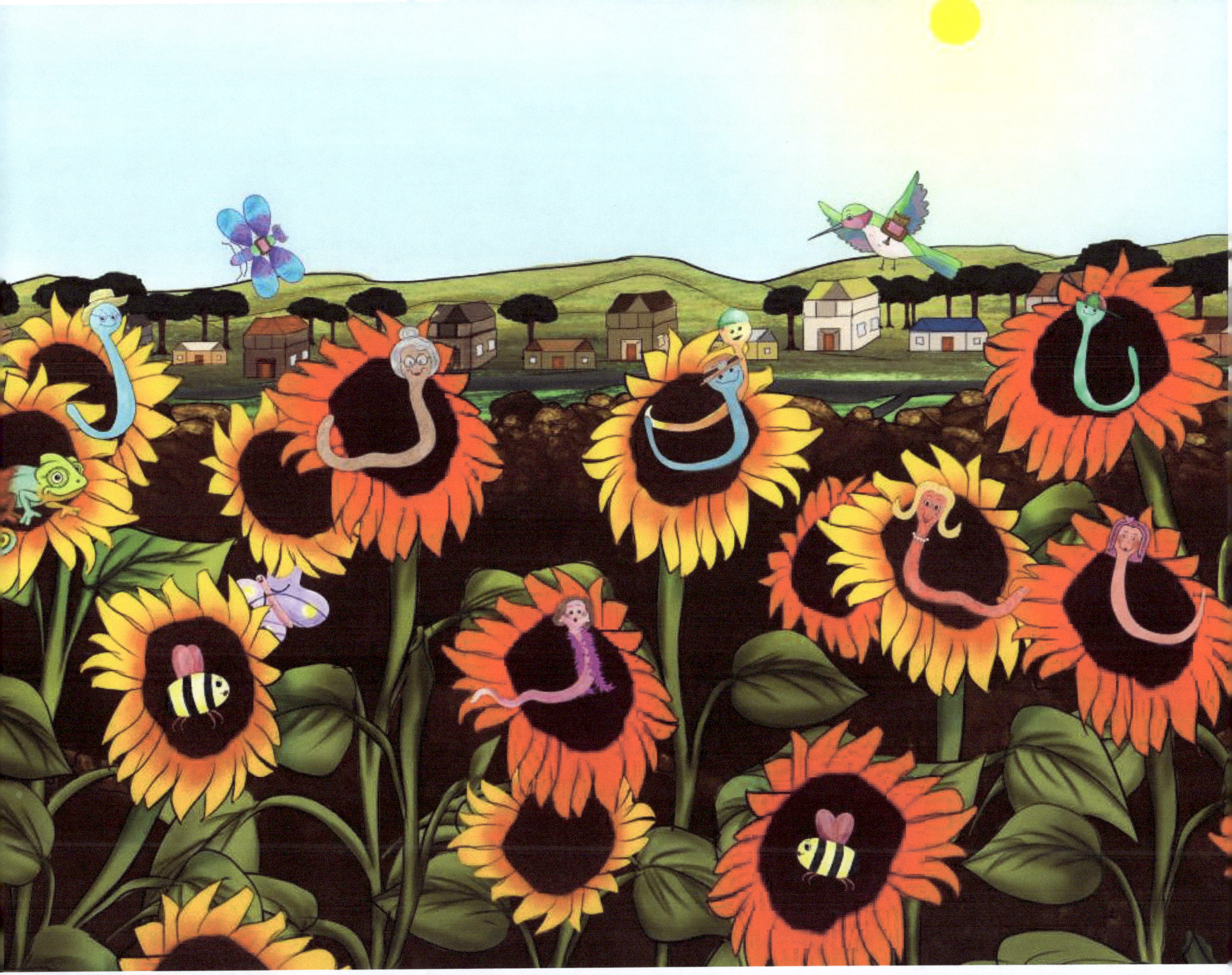

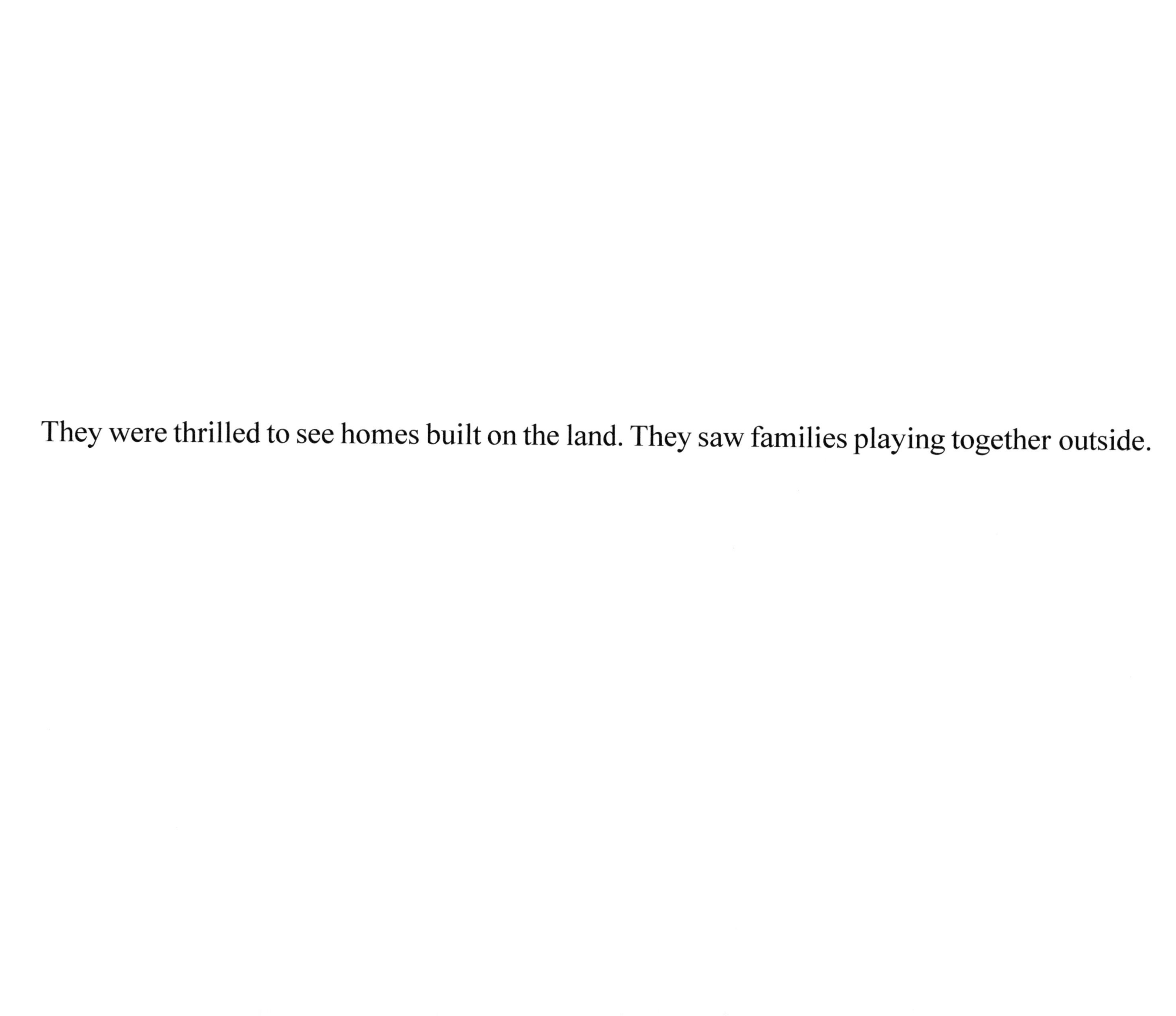

They were thrilled to see homes built on the land. They saw families playing together outside.

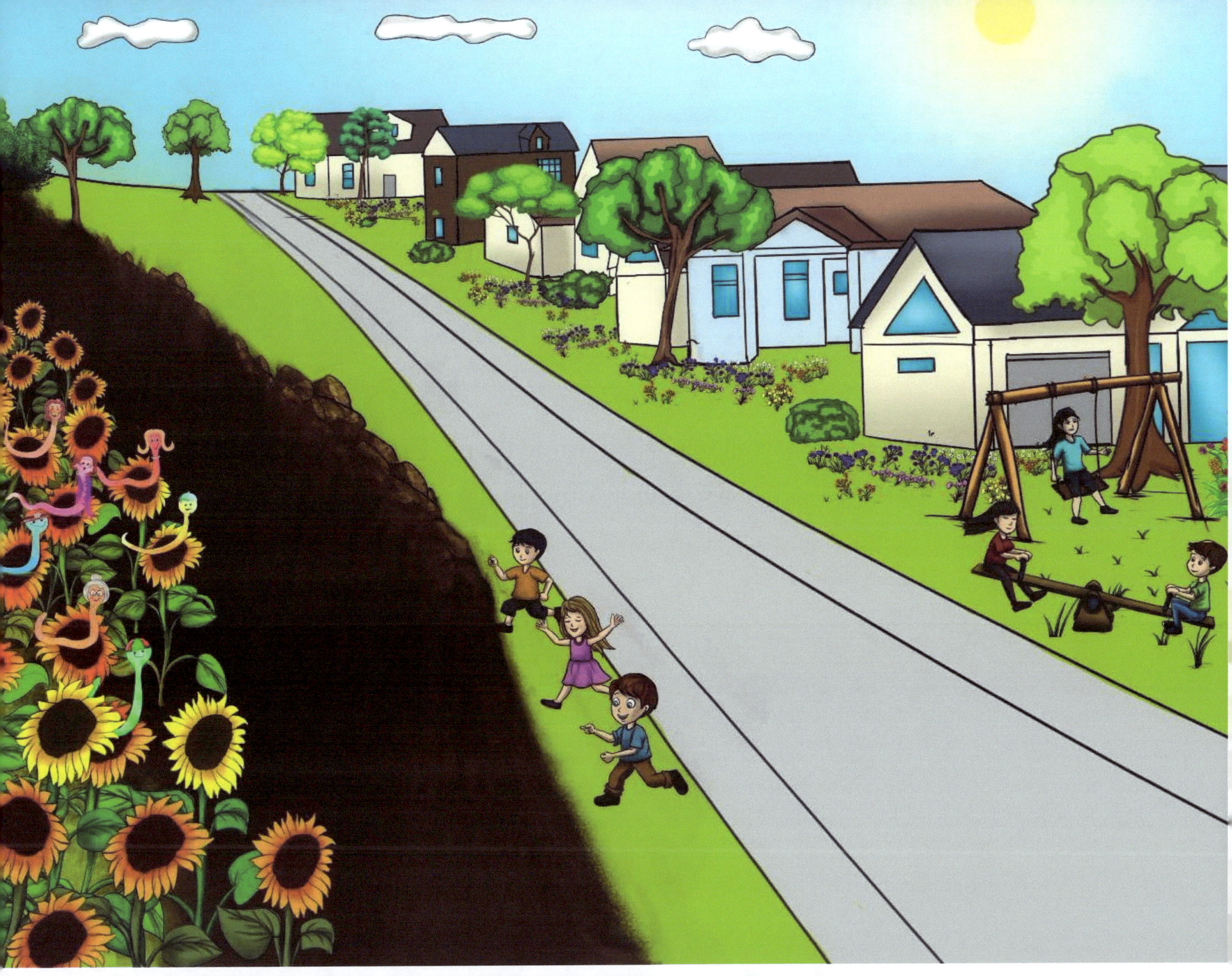

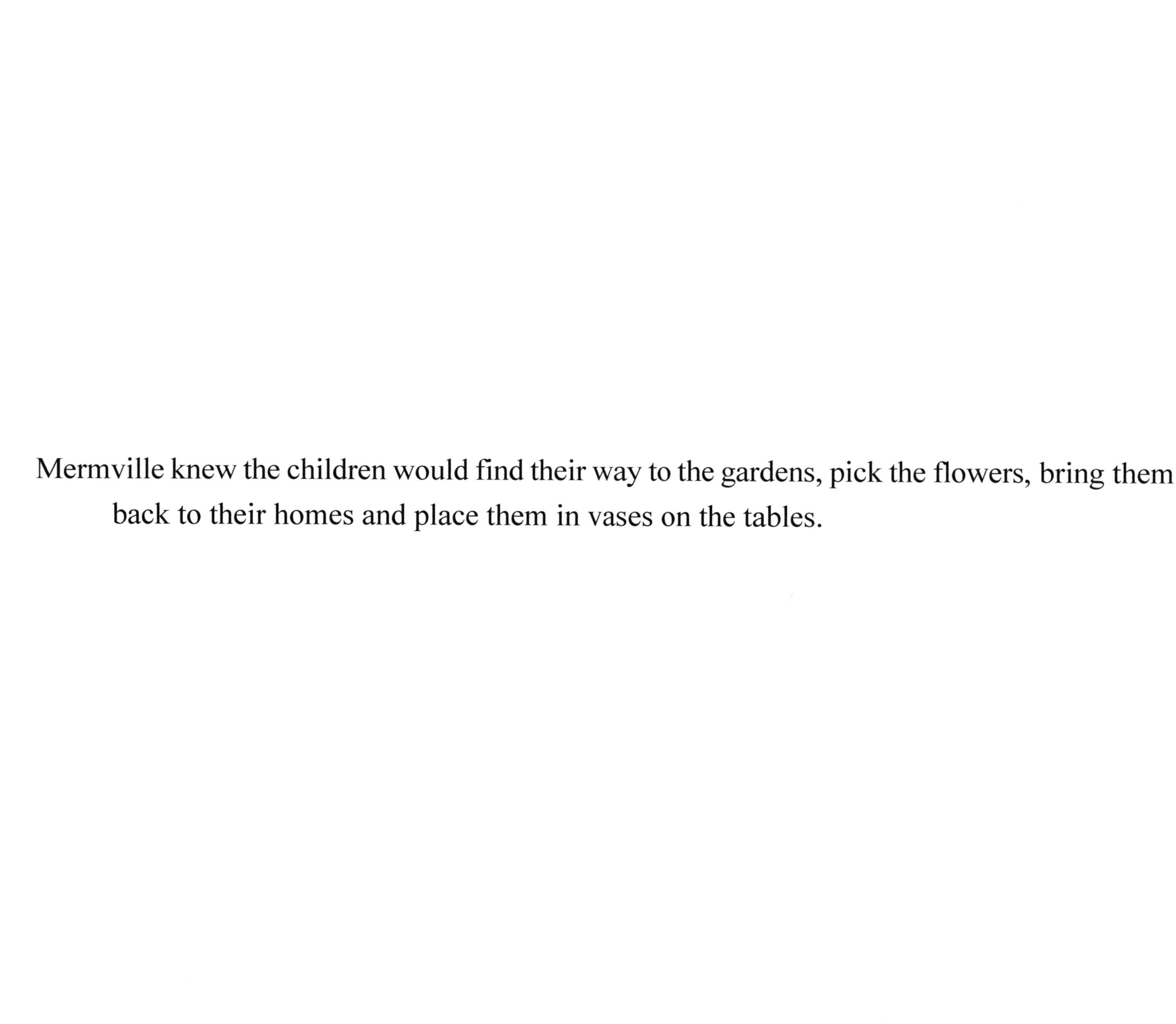

Mermville knew the children would find their way to the gardens, pick the flowers, bring them back to their homes and place them in vases on the tables.

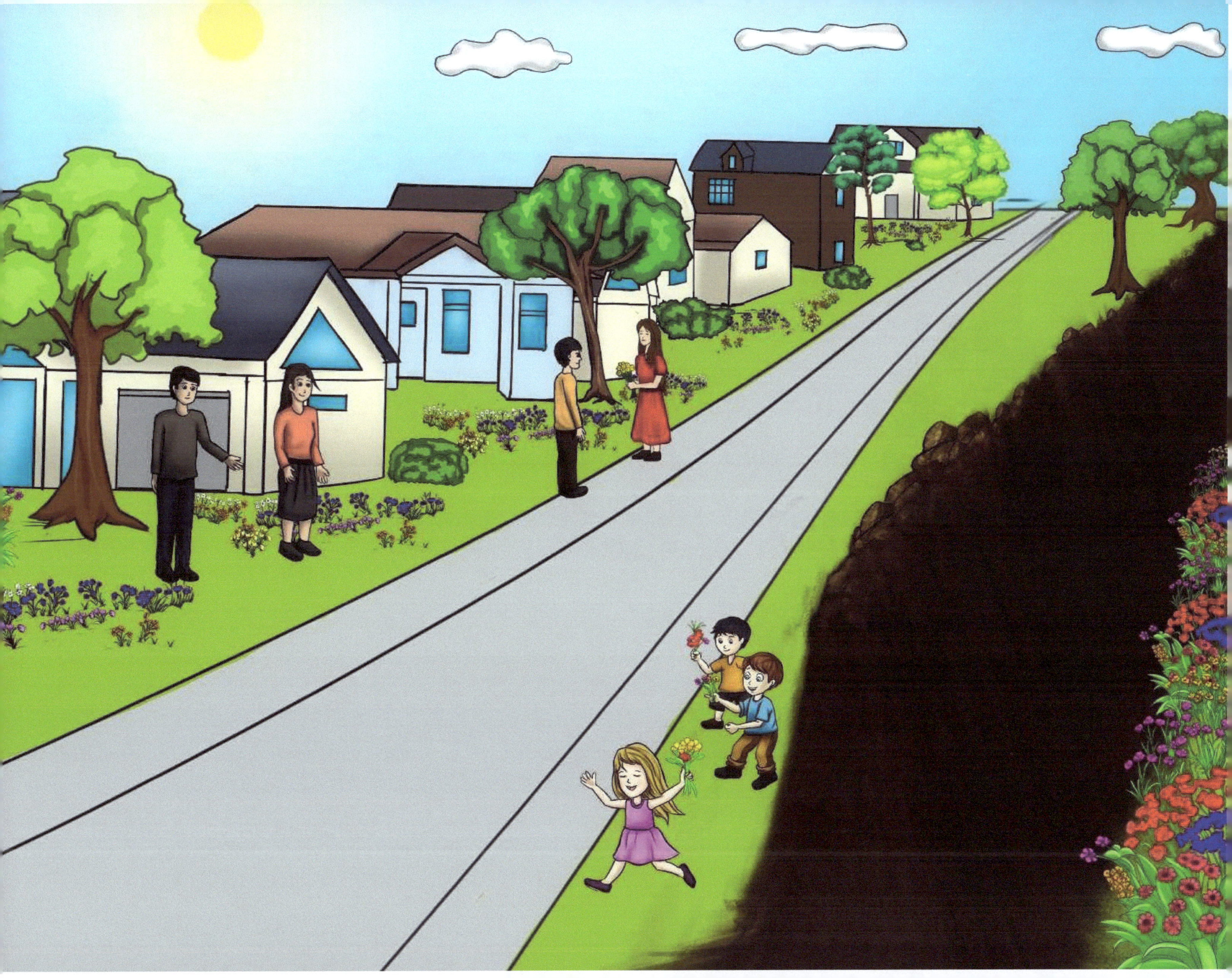

The flowers would share the love messages with the families.

The Mermville community celebrated as everyone had lovingly worked together to create this beautiful garden.

The cycle of life was complete.

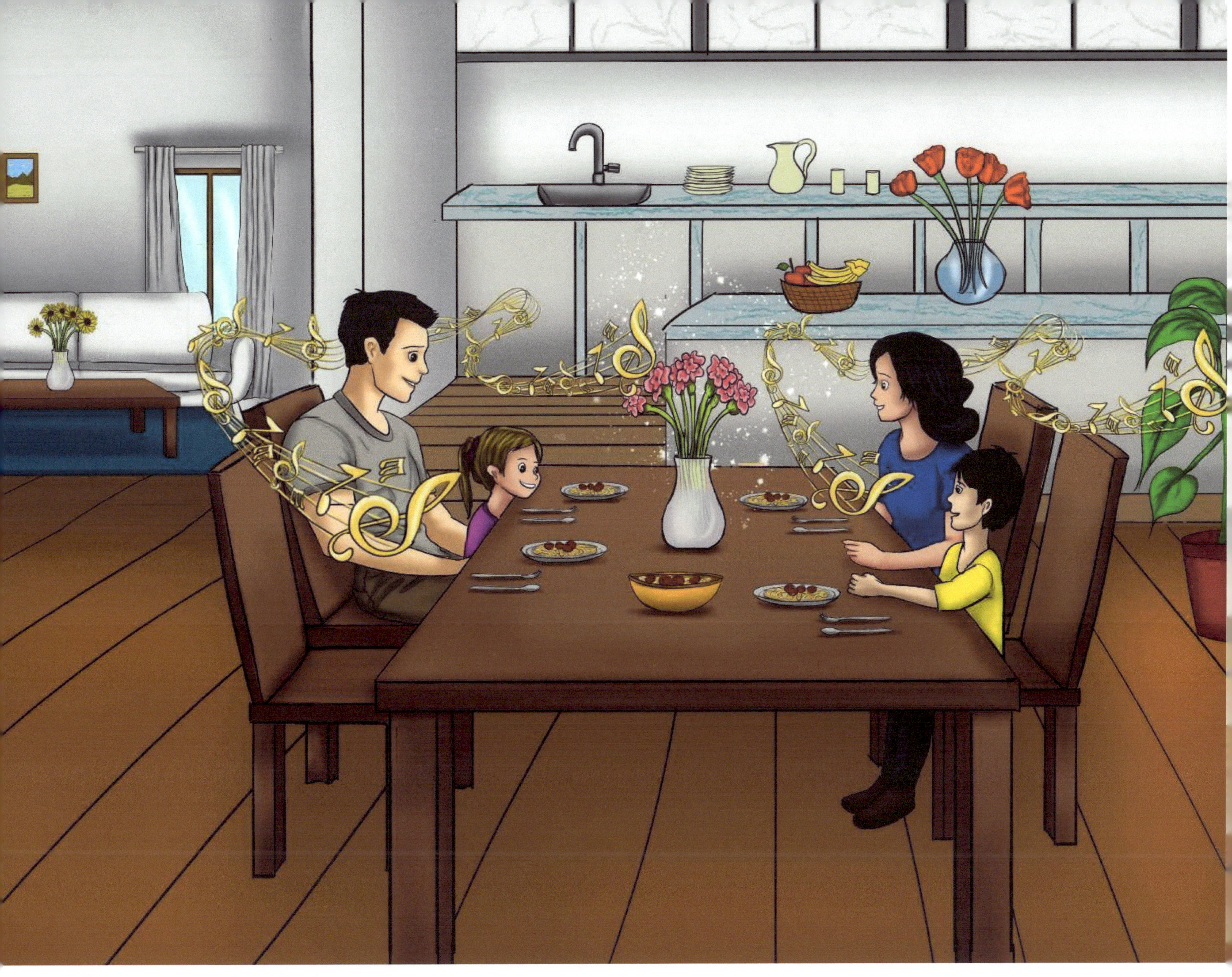

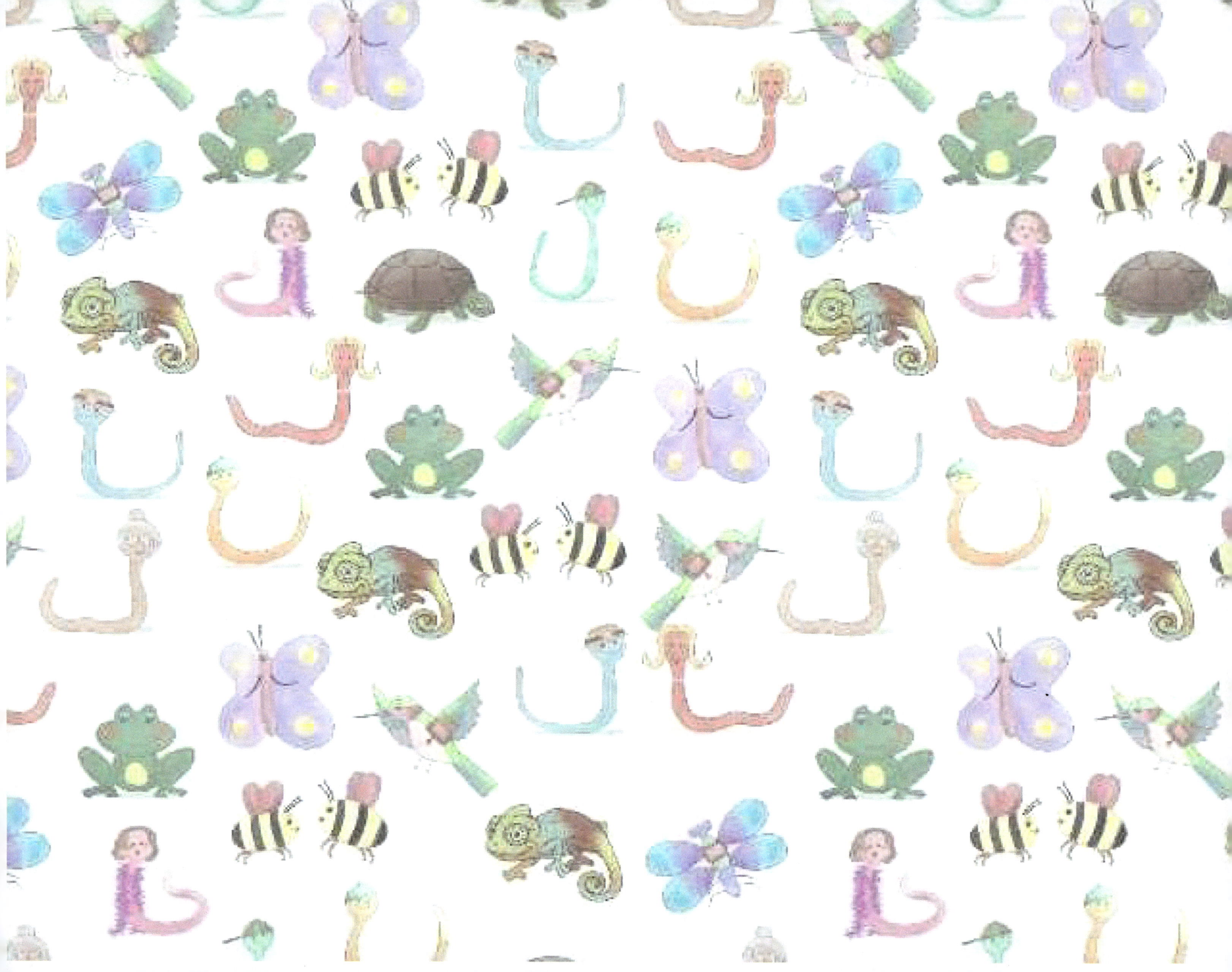